A Note From Rick Renner

I am on a personal quest to see a "revival of the Bible" so people can establish their lives on a firm foundation that will stand strong and endure the test when the end-time storm winds begin to intensify.

In order to experience a revival of the Bible in your personal life, it is important to take time each day to read, receive, and apply its truths to your life. James tells us that if we will continue in the perfect law of liberty — refusing to be forgetful hearers but determined to be doers — we will be blessed in our ways. As you watch or listen to the programs in this series and work through this corresponding study guide, I trust that you will search the Scriptures and allow the Holy Spirit to help you hear something new from God's Word that applies specifically to your life. I encourage you to be a doer of the Word that He reveals to you. Whatever the cost, I assure you — it will be worth it.

> Thy words were found, and I did eat them;
> and thy word was unto me the joy and rejoicing of mine heart:
> for I am called by thy name, O Lord God of hosts.
> — Jeremiah 15:16

Your brother and friend in Jesus Christ,

Rick Renner

Unless otherwise indicated, all scripture quotations are taken from the *King James Version* of the Bible.

How To Use This Study Guide

This five-lesson study guide corresponds to *"Healing the Mind and Emotions of the Oppressed" With Rick Renner* (Renner TV). Each lesson in this study guide covers a topic that is addressed during the program series, with questions and references supplied to draw you deeper into your own private study of the Scriptures on this subject.

To derive the most benefit from this study guide, consider the following:

First, watch or listen to the program prior to working through the corresponding lesson in this guide. (Programs can also be viewed at **renner.org** by clicking on the Media/Archive links.)

Second, take the time to look up the scriptures included in each lesson. Prayerfully consider their application to your own life.

Third, use a journal or notebook to make note of your answers to each lesson's Study Questions and Practical Application challenges.

Fourth, invest specific time in prayer and in the Word of God to consult with the Holy Spirit. Write down the scriptures or insights He reveals to you about being filled with the Spirit and empowered by Him in your daily life.

Finally, take action! Whatever the Lord tells you to do according to His Word, do it.

For added insights on this subject, it is recommended that you obtain Rick Renner's book *Sparkling Gems 1* and *Sparkling Gems 2.* You may also select from Rick's other available resources by placing your order at **renner.org** or by calling 1-800-742-5593.

TOPIC

What Is Oppression?

SCRIPTURES

1. **Acts 10:38** — How God anointed Jesus of Nazareth with the Holy Ghost and with power: who went about doing good, and healing all that were oppressed of the devil; for God was with him.

2. **Luke 4:18** — The Spirit of the Lord is upon me, because he hath anointed me...

3. **2 Corinthians 10:4,5** — (For the weapons of our warfare are not carnal, but mighty through God to the pulling down of strong holds;) Casting down imaginations, and every high thing that exalteth itself against the knowledge of God, and bringing into captivity every thought to the obedience of Christ.

GREEK WORDS

1. "anointed" — χρίω (*chrio*): to rub oil or perfume upon an individual; used in a medical sense for healing ointment; scripturally used to denote the anointing of the Holy Spirit and all the effects He brings to a believer

2. "power" — δύναμις (*dunamis*): power; pictures explosive, superhuman power that comes with enormous energy and produces phenomenal, extraordinary, and unparalleled results; used to depict the full might and power of an advancing army

3. "healing" — ἰάομαι (*iaomai*): to cure; to be doctored; pictures healing power that progressively reverses a condition; denotes healing that comes to pass over a period of time; for this reason, this word is often translated as a treatment, cure, or remedy; depicts a sickness that has been progressively healed rather than instantaneously healed

4. "oppressed" — καταδυναστεύω (*katadunasteuo*): a compound of κατα (kata) and δυνάστης (dunastes); the word κατα (kata) carries the idea of domination; the word δυνάστης (dunastes) depicts a dominating tyrant; when compounded, it pictures the oppressive power of a

wicked tyrant; one who rules over and cruelly tyrannizes his subjects; bullying; cruelty; despotism; dictatorship; oppressiveness; tyranny

5. "devil" — **διάβολος** (*diabolos*): one who repetitiously strikes until successfully penetrating an object to ruin it, affect it, or take it captive; to slander, accuse, or defame; to penetrate by continuous assault; to ensnare with a net

6. "pulling down" — **καθαιρέω** (*kathaireo*): to take down; to disassemble, if needed, bit by bit; to demolish; destroy; to dismantle; to throw down; to knock down, break up, pull apart, and take to pieces, until nothing is left standing; used to picture pulling down the walls of a well defended fortress

7. "strongholds" — **ὀχύρωμα** (*ochuroma*): fortress; castle; citadel; pictures a stronghold with walls fortified to keep outsiders on the outside; a dreadful prison constructed deep inside a fortress that was intended to prevent a hostage or prisoner from escaping; a place of arrest, captivity, confinement, detention, imprisonment, or incarceration

8. "casting down"— **καθαιρέω** (*kathaireo*): to take down; to disassemble, if needed, bit by bit; to demolish; destroy; to dismantle; to throw down; to knock down, break up, pull apart, and take to pieces, until nothing is left standing; used to picture pulling down the walls of a well defended fortress

SYNOPSIS

In this five-part study *Healing the Mind and Emotions of the Oppressed*, the following topics will be examined:

- What Is Oppression?
- Levels of Oppression
- How To Demolish Oppression
- An Extreme Case of Oppression
- Ministering to the Oppressed

The emphasis of this lesson:

Oppression is a tool of the devil to bind up and dominate our lives. We must learn to identify and understand oppression. Once we do, we can learn to walk free.

Moscow is a very old city and the Kremlin is its most ancient section. But if you venture just outside the city, you will find the oldest standing building in Moscow: *The Andronikov Monastery of the Saviour.* Its ancient walls were built in 1357 and have survived plagues, wars, fires, and even the invasion of Napoleon, which occurred in 1812. But in 1917, when the Russian Revolution took place and Soviet powers began to rule the land, the monastery was closed because religion had become illegal. From 1918 to 1922, the monastery became the first shooting gallery in Russia — the site of mass executions. Political prisoners, political opponents, and anyone deemed to be dangerous by the state were incarcerated and shot there. The Andronikov Monastery became a very oppressive place.

What is the true meaning of the word "oppression"? The Bible tells us in Acts 10:38 that "…God anointed Jesus of Nazareth with the Holy Ghost and power and He went about doing good and healing all that were oppressed of the devil." Perhaps you know someone who is oppressed, or maybe you are oppressed in some area of your life. As you embark on this powerful teaching, you will be equipped to recognize, identify, and abolish oppression in your life and in the lives of those around you.

Oppression Defined

What exactly is oppression? First, it is important to understand that oppression is *not* depression. In fact, oppression and depression are not synonymous. Depression can be caused by disappointments, fatigue, diet, a relentless schedule, or it can even be the result of a chemical imbalance. Often, depression can be eliminated by taking a day off, by eating differently, or even by medication. Typically, the source of depression is internal physiologically, or *physical.*

The dictionary meaning of the word "oppression" is *the exercise of authority or power in a burdensome, cruel, or unjust manner.* Oppression is cruel, burdensome, and unjust.

The etymology of the word "oppression" comes from a Latin word, but it basically means *to press upon.* If a person is oppressed, something from the outside is pressing on him or her. "Oppression" means *to overburden, weigh down, overwhelm, or overpower.* When a person is oppressed, he or she feels overpowered by some external force.

"Oppression" also means *to burden with cruel, unjust or unreasonable restraints; to treat with injustice or undue severity; to oppress, afflict, crush, put down, smother, subdue or to torment.*

Synonyms for oppression include: *abuse, brutality, coercion, compulsion, conquering, control, cruelty, dictatorship, domination, force, harshness, harassment, hardness, injustice, iron-handedness, maltreatment, overthrowing, repression, suffering, severity, subjugation, torment, and tyranny.*

In the New Testament, the word "oppression" carries the idea of *tyranny.* It refers to an outside force that is *ruling over, subduing, harassing, conquering, overpowering* and telling the one who's oppressed what to think, what to believe, and what the future will be.

Acts 10:38 uses the word "oppression" in a very significant way. In Acts 10, as Peter began preaching in the household of Cornelius, he began to speak about Jesus.

> **How God anointed Jesus of Nazareth with the Holy Ghost and with power: who went about doing good, and healing all that were oppressed of the devil; for God was with him.**
> **— Acts 10:38**

Anointed

This verse opens with the words, "How God *anointed...*." Praise God for the anointing! The anointing sets people free, and this verse states that Jesus was anointed with the Holy Ghost and power.

The word "anointed" is the Greek word *chiro,* which described *the rubbing of oil or perfume upon an individual.* It was used in a medical sense to depict a healing anointing. However, in the New Testament, it describes the anointing of the Holy Spirit, and its results were available to Jesus — and are also available to every believer. The anointing that was upon Jesus is also available to us today.

The question arises, *When did God anoint Jesus?* God anointed Jesus when He was baptized in the Jordan River and the Holy Spirit came upon Him. Later, when Jesus came to the synagogue in Nazareth, He picked up a scroll, opened it to Isaiah 61 and read these words, which are also recorded in Luke 4:18: "The Spirit of the Lord is upon me; because the Lord hath *anointed* me...."

The word "anoint" (*chiro*) describes what we might call a "hands-on experience." For oil to be applied to the recipient, the anointer didn't simply pour the oil out of the bottle. Instead, he poured the oil into his own hands and then applied the oil to the individual. When Jesus said, "The Spirit of the Lord is upon me because the Lord hath anointed me," it was the equivalent of His saying, "I'm anointed, and the reason I'm anointed is because the Lord has laid His hands on me. The hand of God is on My life, and He has pressed the anointing into Me."

Dunamis Power

Jesus was anointed by God, as spoken by Peter and recorded in Acts 10:38, "How God anointed Jesus of Nazareth with the Holy Ghost and with power…"! In this verse, the word "power" is the Greek word *dunamis*. Some have taught that the word "dynamite" is derived from this word, and that is true, but that is a very superficial meaning for this word "power." Directly from the Greek text, *dunamis* describes *power*, but it pictures *explosive, superhuman power that comes with enormous energy and produces phenomenal, extraordinary, and unparalleled results.*

This same word is used both in the New Testament and in secular literature to describe the full might and power of an advancing army. *Dunamis* is explosive power that comes with unparalleled results when it is released! If you have been anointed with the Holy Ghost and power, you have been anointed to make an advance into a territory to drive back the forces of hell. That is the kind of power you have if you have received the baptism in the Holy Spirit.

When Jesus was anointed, He was anointed with advancing power to drive back the forces of hell. Acts 10:38 continues saying of Jesus, "…Who went about doing good and healing all that were oppressed of the devil."

Doing Good and Healing

The Greek word for "good" is very important. It is the word *euergeteo*, which is comprised of the word *agathos*, meaning *to do good*, and the word *ergao*, meaning *to do*. When compounded, this phrase "doing good" denotes *a benefactor, a philanthropist, or one who financially supports charitable works.* This describes an individual who uses his financial resources to meet the needs of disadvantaged people. When the power of God came on Jesus, not only did He heal people who were sick and oppressed, the power of God also operated in Him to drive back poverty. That is what this phrase "doing good" literally means.

Jesus went about doing good *and* healing. The word "healing" is the Greek word *iaomai*. It is very important to understand the meaning of this word because its meaning indicates that not everything Jesus did was instantaneous. This particular word *iomai* is an old medical term that meant *to cure* or *to be doctored*. It describes healing power that progressively reverses a condition, and it denotes healing that comes to pass over a period of time. For this reason, *iomai* is often translated as *a treatment, a cure,* or *a remedy*. It pictures a sickness that has been progressively healed rather than instantaneously healed.

It is interesting to note that his particular word was used in connection with those who were oppressed of the devil. The word "oppressed" is a very long Greek word, *katadynasteuo* — comprised of the word *kata*, which carries the idea of *something that is coming down or something that is dominating*, and the word *dunamis* or *power*. When compounded, these two words for "oppressed," carry the idea of *domination*, or more precisely, *a dominating tyrant*. It denotes *the oppressive power of a wicked tyrant; one who rules over and cruelly tyrannizes his subjects, bullying them*. It further describes *one who is cruel; one who rules in despotism; a dictator; someone who is oppressive or tyrannical*.

In his discourse in Acts chapter 10, Peter continues by identifying the name of the tyrant as *the devil*. The word "devil" is the Greek word *diabolos*, which depicts *one who repetitiously strikes until successfully penetrating an object to ruin it, affect it, or take it captive*. This word *diabolos* means *to slander, accuse, or defame; to penetrate by continuous assault; to ensnare with a net*.

The devil begins his attack by repeatedly attacking the mind. His intention is to strike the mind so continuously that he finally penetrates it. When the devil penetrates the mind, he begins to take the mind hostage, and like a wicked tyrant, he begins to dictate what a person should feel, think, and believe. He will tell his victims what they can or cannot do and like a wicked tyrant, he subdues them. That outside pressure cruelly oppresses them as it tries to gain inside access and control their life.

Rick's Personal Story of Oppression

In this program, Rick shared a personal testimony of a time he dealt with oppression as a boy.

When I was a boy I dealt with oppression even though I was so young, I didn't really recognize it as oppression. Most of our friends in the church where I grew up participated in sports, and the mindset was that to be a *real man*, you had to be a *sports* man. Sports were highly valued, and our church friends either bowled or played basketball, softball, or baseball. In fact, they participated in anything involving a ball! But guess what? Ricky Renner was not gifted in *any* kind of sports involving a ball. I actually hated every kind of ball sport, and to this day, I don't like any kind of sports that have to do with a ball because it always symbolized failure to me.

As a very young man, voices began to speak to me, saying, *There's something wrong with you. There's something really wrong. You can't compete with the other guys. You cannot do what the other guys can do.* Those thoughts just kept striking my mind and striking my mind, and striking my mind. When I went to school, I tried again to be involved in sports with all the other guys. But, still, I was such a failure when it came to sports. Every day, I would have those feelings of failure reinforced by voices speaking failure to me over and over and over again. This was an early assault on my mind, and because I didn't understand what was happening, I couldn't articulate it or even verbalize it. I knew I was different from the other guys. I liked art, museums, and music, included the symphony. I liked creativity.

I was just wired differently. But the same voice that told me I was a failure for not being good at sports also repeatedly sneered, *You're a freak to like the things you like.* Those voices constantly lambasted me, day in and day out. I can still remember looking into the mirror as a young boy and thinking, *What is wrong with you? There's something really wrong with you.* It wasn't depression; it was an outside oppressive force trying to penetrate my mind and take me hostage.

When I was in the seventh grade I became ill and missed half of the school year. During my absence, a new type of math had been introduced. When I finally returned to school, I had missed half a year of instruction, so I did not understand what was being taught. Not only was I struggling in math, I didn't do well in writing because I had missed so much about English and grammar. Every day I struggled, and as I sat at my desk, I would hear voices speaking to my mind, *There's something wrong with you. You are inferior. You're a failure. You're stupid. You can't understand because you're stupid!* I constantly heard voices accusing me, *You're a failure because you are not athletic. You're a freak because you are so different from other people.*

Even though I really had failed in mathematics, my teacher liked me and graduated me to the next level in school. That may seem like a good thing, but if I didn't understand math in the *seventh* grade, how was I going to understand math in the *eighth* grade? For another entire year, I struggled with mathematics with that relentless voice speaking to me, *There's something wrong with you. You're just stupid!* But that year, my eighth-grade teacher also liked me and passed me into the ninth grade.

When I entered ninth grade, we were going to study algebra. Well, my algebra teacher was so old that she had also been my *father's* algebra teacher! Unfortunately, when my father was a child, she did not like him. During my first day in class, as this teacher was taking roll, she came to my name and said, "Ricky Renner."

I responded, "Here." She asked, "Is your father Ronald Renner?" I answered, "Yes, that's my father." I vividly remember her face as she pulled her glasses down to the end of her nose. She peered at me behind those thick lenses. Then she pushed her glasses back up onto her face and said matter-of-factly, "Stupid. In this class your name is *Stupid.* Any child of Ronald Renner is *stupid, stupid, stupid* — and that is your name in this class."

Notice what was happening. The devil was telling me I was a stupid failure and a freak. And now he was able to bring in reinforcements through this woman. He began to use someone who was an authority figure, with the power of influence, to reinforce the lies he had already been telling me.

Then when the other students heard what the teacher had called me, they thought it was hysterical and they all began to call me Stupid. When I walked through the hallway at school, I would hear, "Hey Stupid! Hey Stupid, where are you going?" Every day when that teacher called the roll in class, she would call everyone else by their actual name, but as soon as she came to my name, she would call out, "Stupid Renner." And every time, I would compliantly answer, "Here." If I raised my hand to ask a question, she would respond, "Yes, Stupid. Can somebody please help Stupid?"

I was labeled Stupid in that class and it spread to the hallways and the campus of that school.

The devil — *diabolos* — was striking and striking and striking to penetrate my mind so I would believe the lie that I was stupid, a failure, a freak, and that there was something really wrong with me. The devil was an outsider and a cruel dictator — an absolute tyrant trying to subdue, conquer, and dominate my young life. He was trying to convince me to believe the lie, because whatever we believe about ourselves becomes our reality. The devil knew if I began to believe what I was hearing, that lie would have eventually become my reality, and I would fail in life.

The devil wants us to believe his lies because if he can deceive us into believing a lie, that lie will become our reality. Oppression will leave the mental and spiritual realms and it will become a reality in all of life.

Even though the devil was in pursuit of my destruction through his persistent lies, when I was 14 years old, I gloriously received the baptism in the Holy Spirit, and those attacks ceased. When I received the baptism in the Holy Spirit, the power of God came on me, the devil's mission was aborted. All of those attacks stopped and drove that darkness out of my life.

The devil is a tyrant and he wants to lord over people. He wants to tell us what to think, what to believe, and his goal is to feed us lie after lie trying to get us to take the bait and believe him. Then with that false mindset, we begin acting accordingly and our view of life and of ourselves changes radically for the worse.

That is what oppression is and how it operates.

STUDY QUESTIONS

Study to shew thyself approved unto God, a workman that needeth not to be ashamed, rightly dividing the word of truth.
— 2 Timothy 2:15

1. People often believe that *depression* and *oppression* are synonymous, but they are not. List three differences between depression and oppression.

2. Most of us have experienced both *depression* and *oppression* in our lifetime. Think of an instance in which you dealt with depression. Were you able to identify it as depression, and if so, what steps did you take to overcome the depression?

3. Has there been a time in your life when the enemy has tried to convince you of a lie? Perhaps you are still believing his lie in an area of your life today. What will you do to dismantle that lie?

4. When Jesus said, "The Spirit of the Lord is upon Me because the Lord has anointed Me," in essence He was saying, "The hand of God is on My life and *He has pressed the anointing into Me.*" Think of this statement in terms of your own life. What are some practical steps you can take to walk more fully in the anointing the Lord has pressed into *your* life?

5. Explain why the meaning of "healing" (*iomai*) in Acts 10:38 so important to understand concerning the ministry of Jesus.

PRACTICAL APPLICATION

But be ye doers of the word, and not hearers only, deceiving your own selves.
— James 1:2

1. Think of an area in your life where the devil has tried to penetrate your mind and emotions. Find one scripture or more that can help you combat this attack with the truth of God's Word.

TOPIC

Levels of Oppression

SCRIPTURES

1. **Acts 10:38** — How God anointed Jesus of Nazareth with the Holy Ghost and with power: who went about doing good, and healing all that were oppressed of the devil; for God was with him.

2. **2 Corinthians 10:4,5** — (For the weapons of our warfare are not carnal, but mighty through God to the pulling down of strong holds;) Casting down imaginations, and every high thing that exalteth itself against the knowledge of God, and bringing into captivity every thought to the obedience of Christ.

GREEK WORDS

1. "oppressed" — **καταδυναστεύω** (*katadunasteuo*): a compound of **κατα** (kata) and **δυνάστης** (dunastes); the word **κατα** (kata) carries the idea of domination; the word **δυνάστης** (dunastes) depicts a dominating tyrant; when compounded, it pictures the oppressive power of a wicked tyrant; one who rules over and cruelly tyrannizes his subjects; bullying; cruelty; despotism; dictatorship; oppressiveness; tyranny

2. "devil" — **διάβολος** (*diabolos*): one who repetitiously strikes until successfully penetrating an object to ruin it, affect it, or take it captive; to slander, accuse, or defame; to penetrate by continuous assault; to ensnare with a net

3. "mighty" — **δυνατὰ** (*dunata*): from **δύναμις** (dunamis), power; pictures explosive, superhuman power that comes with enormous energy and produces phenomenal, extraordinary, and unparalleled results; used to depict the full might and power of an advancing army

4. "pulling down" — **καθαιρέω** (*kathaireo*): to take down; to disassemble, if needed, bit by bit; to demolish; destroy; to dismantle; to throw down; to knock down, break up, pull apart, and take to pieces, until nothing is left standing; used to picture pulling down the walls of a well defended fortress

5. "strongholds" — ὀχύρωμα (*ochuroma*): fortress; castle; citadel; pictures a stronghold with walls fortified to keep outsiders on the outside; a dreadful prison constructed deep inside a fortress that was intended to prevent a hostage or prisoner from escaping; a place of arrest, captivity, confinement, detention, imprisonment, or incarceration

6. "casting down" — καθαιρέω (*kathaireo*): to take down; to disassemble, if needed, bit by bit; to demolish; destroy; to dismantle; to throw down; to knock down, break up, pull apart, and take to pieces, until nothing is left standing; used to picture pulling down the walls of a well defended fortress

7. "imaginations" — λογισμός (*logismos*): where we get the word logic, as in logical thinking; used to denote thoughts or reasoning in the mind

SYNOPSIS

The Andronikov Monastery in Moscow is located in one of the most ancient areas of the city outside the Kremlin. Built in 1357, it is the oldest standing building in the city of Moscow. Built to be a monastery, it served as a monastery for hundreds of years. It withstood fires, invasions, raids, plagues, diseases, and even the invasion of Napoleon in 1812. But finally in 1917, at the end of the Bolshevik Revolution (also known as the Russian Revolution), the monastery was officially closed because religion became illegal. An anti-God regime came to power and the Andronikov Monastery became a concentration camp. Those who disagreed with the government were housed there and those who were considered to be political opponents were incarcerated there. From 1918 to 1922, it became a place of mass executions and, to this day, no one knows how many people were actually executed behind these ancient walls.

Finally, in 1991, the Monastery was returned to the Russian Orthodox Church and is once again a working monastery. It is a museum, a church, and it houses some of the most fabulous Russian icons from the entire history of the Russian Orthodox Church. But again, from 1918 to 1922, this was a place of horrible and horrific oppression.

Oppression is a terrible thing, and there are many levels of oppression. There is political oppression, spiritual oppression, mental oppression, and so many other forms of oppression.

The emphasis of this lesson:

The devil has a strategy to build strongholds in our minds, but we have been given weapons to demolish every lie. As we learn to identify the seven levels of oppression and two types of strongholds, we will be better equipped to defeat the enemy and walk in freedom.

In our last lesson, we examined the definition of oppression, how it operates, and how it enters into the lives of people. We also looked at a real-life example of how oppression was at work in Rick Renner's young life.

In review, oppression is not depression. Depression can be caused by disappointment, fatigue, stress, schedule, or diet and can typically be remedied by taking a day off, getting into a better environment, making a change in diet, or even taking medication. But oppression is something else entirely. Oppression is an exterior, spiritual force.

The meaning of the word "oppression" is *the exercise of authority or power that is burdensome, cruel, and unjust.* The etymology of this word further reveals its meaning: *to press upon, to press against, to overburden, to weight down, to overwhelm, to overpower; to burden with cruel, unjust or unreasonable restraints. To treat with severity, to oppress, afflict crush, put down, smother, subdue, or torment.*

When oppression is at work, there is a tormenting exterior force that is pressing against an individual emotionally or spiritually, trying to subdue, conquer, and overcome that person. Oppression is a very spiritual force. Synonyms for oppression include: *abuse, brutality, coercion, compulsion, conquering, control, cruelty, despotism, dictatorship, domination, force, harshness, harassment, hardness, injustice, an iron hand that is trying to rule you spiritually, maltreatment, overthrowing, repression, suffering, severity, subjugation, torment, and tyranny.*

As we have discussed previously, in Acts 10:38, Peter is preaching and says, "How God anointed Jesus of Nazareth with the Holy Ghost and with power: who went about doing good, and healing all that were *oppressed of the devil*; for God was with him." Oppression comes from the devil, and it is an exterior pressure trying to subdue, smother, dominate, and rule you like a tyrant.

The devil will plant his lies and begin pounding a person's mind or emotions. He strikes repetitiously, continuously *striking and striking and striking* until he finally wears the person down, and his lies penetrate his mind or emotions. He floods that person's mind with his lies and takes him captive. From that point forward, the devil rules that individual like a tyrant.

Seven Levels of Oppression

There are seven levels of oppression that will be identified in this lesson.

Level Number One: *A Personal Attack*

The *first* level of oppression is a personal attack against the mind and emotions. Remember, the devil is *diabolos*, and is the one striking and striking and striking the mind. Rick recalled that when the devil repeatedly spoke to his mind, *You're a failure. You're a freak. You're stupid. Something is wrong with you,* he was striking his mind ruthlessly and continuously. From a very young age, Rick was targeted. The devil's intention was penetration of Rick's mind to gain access to and control over his thoughts, emotions, and belief system so he could ultimately destroy him and God's purpose for his life.

Level Number Two: *Reinforcements*

During the *second* level of oppression, the devil sends reinforcements to fortify his mental and emotional attack. In other words, the devil will use people to corroborate the lies he is speaking to you. In Rick's case, Rick believed he was a failure at sports and that there was something wrong with him. One way the devil tried to reinforce that thinking in Rick's young mind was through a baseball coach who mocked him publicly, telling him he was stupid and a failure — which only confirmed to Rick what he was already feeling and being harassed with.

That is what the devil does; he brings in reinforcements through people who will yield to him to support what you are already hearing from him.

Level Number Three: *Life Experiences and Disappointments*

In stage *three* of oppression, the devil uses negative life experiences and disappointments to fortify his deceptive lies. Experience after experience in Rick's life convinced him that what he was believing and what he was hearing was the truth. He was not doing well in math; he was not doing well in English, which is amazing because today he is a prolific author of many books and publications. It was if the enemy knew certain things about Rick's life and was attempting to sabotage him and abort his divine calling.

Notice the pattern:

1. A lie.
2. Reinforcements for the lie being spoken to the mind.
3. Life experiences and disappointments further fortifying wrong thoughts and feelings.

Level Number Four: *Influential Voices*

In stage *four* of oppression, influential voices bolster the intensity of the devil's attack. As previously recounted, when Rick entered ninth grade, he had a teacher who disliked his dad. On his first day of class, he innocently showed up and the bombardment began. Rick had not wronged that teacher, yet when she realized who his father was — whom she didn't like — she voiced, "Any son of Ronald Renner is stupid and in this class. And that is your new name: *Stupid* Renner." Every day when she called the roll, she called everyone else by his or her given name. But she got to Rick's name, she called out, "Stupid Renner," to which he would dutifully respond, "Here."

Because an *influential voice* was now speaking to him, repeating exactly the same lie the devil had been speaking, Rick was victimized by an intensifying of that attack.

The ninth-grade students had also taken job-placement tests that year. After Rick took his job-placement test, he was called in for his interview by test administrators — more voices of authority — to tell him how he should plan his future education and vocation. Two different counselors said to him, "Ricky, you have no future. Mentally, you don't have what is needed to go to college or pursue higher levels of education. We would encourage you to think about digging ditches or maybe helping to build roads — doing something manual because mentally you will never be able to handle anything higher."

The devil was trying to bolster the intensity of the attack on Rick's life through influential voices — experts. The enemy had brought the teacher, his fellow students, and, finally, two job-placement counselors to reinforce his lies. On top of that, the devil was speaking lies to him personally, striking his mind repeatedly in order to penetrate his mind and thoughts to have access and complete domination.

Level Number Five: *Negative Faith*

In the *fifth* level of oppression, negative faith is released into the lie working in the mind and emotions. Jesus clearly taught that whatever we believe is what we receive. The devil's purpose is to inundate our minds with a lie until we hear it so many times, the lie begins to become "truth" to us. In other words, we begin to believe we're stupid or a failure, etc. We begin to believe that there is something wrong with us, and what we believe about ourselves, our faith will empower to become a reality.

What you believe is so important. If you believe a lie, your believing will empower that lie, and it will become your reality. Conversely, if you believe *the truth*, *the truth* will become your reality. Whatever you believe becomes your reality. If you release negative faith in a lie, you will empower that lie, which leads us to stage number six.

Level Number Six: *What Is Believed Becomes a Reality*

When lies leave the mental realm and enter the physical realm, whatever you have believed becomes your reality. If you believe the lie that you are stupid, you become stupid. If you believe you are a failure, you become a failure. If you believe you are a freak, you become a freak. When we believe the lie, our faith is released into it. When we accept the lie, it leaves the mental and emotional realm and enters the real, physical realm.

Level Number Seven: *Domination for a Lifetime*

The ultimate aim of the enemy is to take us hostage so he can dominate us for the rest of our lives. That did not happen to Rick because he received the baptism in the Holy Spirit, and it set him free.

If you have never received the baptism in the Holy Spirit, call RENNER Ministries, and we will pray with you. The power of the Holy Ghost will set you free.

The Weapons of Our Warfare

In Second Corinthians 10:4, the apostle Paul teaches us how we can deal with mental lies and oppression.

> **For the weapons of our warfare are not carnal, but mighty through God to the pulling down of strong holds.**
> **2 Corinthians 10:4**

According to this verse, we have spiritual weapons, and they are *mighty!* The word "mighty" is the Greek word *dunatos,* from the Greek word *dunamis,* which pictures *superhuman explosive power with enormous energy.* It describes *the full might of an advancing army.* Our weapons are not weak; we have mighty weapons. This verse says *they are mighty through God to the pulling down of strongholds!*

The phrase "pulling down" is a strong word. The Greek word for this phrase means to *take down* or *to disassemble.* If you have entertained wrong thoughts for a long time, you must disassemble them, take them down. If necessary, those thoughts need to be taken apart bit by bit. "Pulling down" means *to demolish, destroy, dismantle, throw down, knock down, break up, pull apart, and take to pieces until nothing is left standing.* It is used to picture the pulling down of the walls of a well-defended fortress.

The Greek word for "stronghold" is *ochuroma,* which literally describes a castle or fortress with walls fortified to keep an outsider on the outside. The same word describes a dreadful prison constructed deep inside a fortress intended to prevent a hostage or prisoner from escaping. It is a place of arrest, captivity, confinement, detention, imprisonment, or incarceration. When you have a mental stronghold, it is like a castle has been built in your brain. The devil, like a wicked king, moves into the castle. From this high place in your life, from your mind and your emotions, he begins dictating to you, subduing you, telling you what to believe, what to feel, and what will happen to you. He builds that fortress so securely in your mind and emotions, it traps you like you are in a prison. Even worse, others who try to help you cannot seem to penetrate because the walls of the lie are so thick that when they tell you the truth, you cannot hear them. The truth cannot penetrate because you have been insulated by a lie. The Bible says we have the power to dismantle, disassemble, and if need be, bit by bit begin to take apart those lies that are in our minds.

Verse 5 of Second Corinthians 10 says, "Casting down imaginations...." The word "imaginations" describes the place where strongholds are found. It is the Greek word *logismos,* from which the word *logic* is derived. This word is used to denote the logical thinking or reasoning of the mind.

Two Kinds of Strongholds

There are two kinds of strongholds, which the Bible calls "imaginations."

1. Logical Strongholds

Sometimes, logical strongholds are more difficult to recognize because they are logical. For example, a person might say, "I can't do everything God is asking me to do because I don't have the money to do it." Logically, that might be accurate in terms of facts, but his logic is restricting his or her obedience. It is a wrong imagination because he or she is bound by logic.

2. Illogical Strongholds

It would seem that an illogical stronghold would be the easiest to identify, but that is not always the case. An example of an illogical stronghold is a skinny person who believes he or she is fat. Every time that person looks in the mirror, he sees a fat person and hears a voice saying, *You have so many rolls. You are so fat!* The truth may actually be that the person is so underweight that he needs to eat! But an illogical stronghold is controlling him. What he believes of the lie has become reality to him because the penetrating voice of the enemy has been speaking a lie to him for so long.

A logical stronghold will keep you bound; it will keep you in prison and stop you from obeying God and living an exciting, adventurous life of faith. An illogical stronghold will bind you up in a wrong self-image; it will tie you up in a lie that is trying to dominate your life. But according to the apostle Paul, we have weapons that are mighty and explosively powerful. And when they are released, the full might of an advancing army is dispensed. With the weapons of God, we can pull down, disassemble, and take apart those strongholds bit by bit, if necessary, until we have finally disassembled those lies in our heads and can walk permanently free!

STUDY QUESTIONS

Study to shew thyself approved unto God, a workman that needeth not to be ashamed, rightly dividing the word of truth.
— 2 Timothy 2:15

1. Write the progression of the devil's strategy to dominate our minds by listing the seven levels of oppression and a brief description of each. Is there an area in your life where you can identify with one of these levels of oppression? What will you do to pull down the walls that seem to be being erected in your life?

2. Most of us have dealt with logical and illogical strongholds in our lives. List one logical and one illogical stronghold you have entertained in the past. How did you overcome?

PRACTICAL APPLICATION

> **But be ye doers of the word, and not hearers only,**
> **deceiving your own selves.**
> **—James 1:22**

1. The devil will always try to find ways to gain control of our mind and emotions. Make a plan to fortify yourself against his attacks by finding specific scriptures that dissemble the lies he is trying to reinforce in your life.

LESSON 3

TOPIC

How To Demolish Oppression

SCRIPTURES

1. **2 Corinthians 10:4** — For the weapons of our warfare are not carnal, but mighty through God to the pulling down of strong holds.

2. **Ephesians 6:14-18** — Stand therefore, having your loins girt about with truth, and having on the breastplate of righteousness; And your feet shod with the preparation of the gospel of peace; Above all, taking the shield of faith, wherewith ye shall be able to quench all the fiery darts of the wicked. And take the helmet of salvation, and the sword of the Spirit, which is the word of God: Praying always with all prayer and supplication in the Spirit...

3. **2 Corinthians 10:5** — Casting down imaginations, and every high thing that exalteth itself against the knowledge of God, and bringing into captivity every thought to the obedience of Christ.

4. **Acts 10:38** — How God anointed Jesus of Nazareth with the Holy Ghost and with power: who went about doing good, and healing all that were oppressed of the devil; for God was with him.

GREEK WORDS

1. "weapons" — ὅπλα (*hopla*): from ὅπλον (*hoplon*), armor, weapons; used in Ephesians 6:14-18 to depict the whole armor of God that potentially belongs to every believer

2. "warfare" — στρατεία (*strateia*): the word for a well-planned, strategic attack; derived from στρατεύομαι (*strateuomai*), which depicts strategic warfare; includes a line of attack, methods to be used in an attack, and the route chosen to carry out a debilitating assault

3. "carnal" — σαρκικός (*sarkikos*): fleshly; natural; whatever is derived from the fleshly, natural, or material world

4. "mighty" — δυνατὰ (*dunata*): from δύναμις (*dunamis*), power; pictures explosive, superhuman power that comes with enormous energy and produces phenomenal, extraordinary, and unparalleled results; used to depict the full might and power of an advancing army

5. "through God" — Τῷ Θεῷ (*to Theo*): through God; through the instrumentality of God; through a partnership with God

6. "to" — πρός (*pros*): to; toward; face to face; a confrontation

7. "pulling down" — καθαιρέω (*kathaireo*): to take down; to disassemble, if needed, bit by bit; to demolish; destroy; to dismantle; to throw down; to knock down, break up, pull apart, and take to pieces, until nothing is left standing; used to picture pulling down the walls of a well defended fortress

8. "strongholds" — ὀχύρωμα (*ochuroma*): fortress; castle; citadel; pictures a stronghold with walls fortified to keep outsiders on the outside; a dreadful prison constructed deep inside a fortress that was intended to prevent a hostage or prisoner from escaping; a place of arrest, captivity, confinement, detention, imprisonment, or incarceration

9. "casting down" — καθαιρέω (*kathaireo*): to take down; to disassemble, if needed, bit by bit; to demolish; destroy; to dismantle; to throw down; to knock down, break up, pull apart, and take to pieces, until nothing is left standing; used to picture pulling down the walls of a well defended fortress

10. "imaginations" — λογισμός (*logismos*): where we get the word logic, as in logical thinking; used to denote thoughts or reasoning in the mind

11. "every" — π ᾶν (*pan*): all; an all-encompassing word, meaning nothing excluded

12. "high thing" — ὕψωμα (*hupsoma*): barrier; bulwark; presumption

13. "exalted itself" — ἐπαίρω (*epairo*): to lift up; depicts a haughty, arrogant, prideful rising; to wrongfully assert

14. "against the knowledge of God" — κατὰ τῆς γνώσεως τοῦ Θεοῦ (*kata tes gnoseos tou theou*): the word κατά (*kata*) means against; in this phrase, it means to dominate, quash, pull under its control, or to subdue; the words τῆς γνώσεως τοῦ Θεοῦ (*tes gnoseos tou theou*) depicts knowledge that finds its origin in God or absolutely clear knowledge that comes from God; hence, this phrase depicts a war against all knowledge that comes from God

15. "bringing into captivity" — αἰχμαλωτίζω (*aichmalotidzo*): pictures a soldier who has captured an enemy and now leads him into captivity with the point of a sharpened spear thrust into the flesh of his back; the captive doesn't dare move or resist, but is silent, submissive, and non-resistant; to lead into captivity; to force one into obedience, submission, and slavery; to bring under control

16. "every" — πᾶν (*pan*): all; an all-encompassing word, meaning nothing excluded

17. "thought" — νόημα (*noema*): thought; insinuation; includes emotions

18. "obedience" — ὑπακούω (*hupakouo*): from ὑπό (*hupo*) and ακούω (*akouo*); the word ὑπό (*hupo*) means under and implies a subservient position; the word ακούω (*akouo*) means to listen: pictures who is submitted, who listens willingly or by force, and who obeys what he hears either willing or by compulsion, duress, or pressure

19. "Christ" — χριστός (*christos*): Christ; The One Who Is Anointed; the anointing

20. "power" — δύναμις (*dunamis*): power; pictures explosive, superhuman power that comes with enormous energy and produces phenomenal, extraordinary, and unparalleled results; used to depict the full might and power of an advancing army

21. "oppressed" — καταδυναστεύω (*katadunasteuo*): a compound of κατα (*kata*) and δυνάστης (*dunastes*); the word κατα (*kata*) carries the idea of domination; the word δυνάστης (*dunastes*) depicts a dominating tyrant; when compounded, it pictures the oppressive power of a wicked tyrant; one who rules over and cruelly tyrannizes his subjects; bullying; cruelty; despotism; dictatorship; oppressiveness; tyranny

22. "devil" — διάβολος (*diabolos*): one who repetitiously strikes until successfully penetrating an object to ruin it, affect it, or take it captive;

to slander, accuse, or defame; to penetrate by continuous assault; to ensnare with a net

SYNOPSIS

Moscow is such an ancient city, the earliest remembrances of it date back to 1147. By the time the Novospassky Monastery was built, Moscow was nearly 300 years old. This is a very renowned monastery. Many famous people have been buried here. For example, the mother of the first female Romanov Tsar is buried at the Novospassky Monastery. Another very reputable character also buried at this monastery is Princess Tarakanova. She claimed to be the only surviving daughter of the Empress Elizabeth, who was the daughter of Peter the Great. However, it was discovered she was a fraud, so she was held as a prisoner and later died and was buried here.

In 1640, when Michael Romanov came to power, he began to embellish the monastery and built a family altar to the Roman gods. The monastery also survived wars and the invasion of Napoleon. But in 1917, the Bolshevik Revolution occurred and the Bolsheviks came to power. The Bolsheviks were communists and atheists; they did not believe in God. When they came to power, the Novospassky Monastery was officially closed, as were nearly all religious sites in the entire land of Russia. What a tragic time it was for the Russian people. The monastery was converted into a concentration camp. That place, which had once been such a holy and historic site, became one of the first shooting monasteries in Moscow — a place of mass executions. People who were incarcerated never left there alive.

Finally, in 1930, the monastery fell into dilapidation, as did nearly all religious sites in Russia. Because the Soviet authorities did not believe in God, no money was spent on the maintenance of historic buildings. Religion was nearly discarded, and the building fell into such dilapidation that the decision was made to bomb and totally demolish it. The only thing that stopped its total destruction was the outbreak of World War II. However, in 1991, everything in Russia changed. God moved into Russia's political system. He began to pour His Spirit out upon the land of Russia, and as a result, this building was officially returned to the Russian Orthodox Church. From that time until now, the Novospassky Monastery has been a working monastery.

In the early years of the Soviet Union, the Novospassky Monastery was a place of torture, imprisonment, oppression, and terrible executions. Oppression is such a horrible thing. At that time, oppression did not just occur physically; oppression is spiritual and was felt throughout the entire land of Russia.

The emphasis of this lesson:

We have been given powerful weapons and a winning strategy to pull down fortresses built by the devil. In this lesson, you will learn what they are and how to implement them.

Oppression: A Wicked Tyrant

In our study of *Healing the Mind and Emotions of the Oppressed*, we have defined oppression, learned about the seven levels of oppression, and have begun to explore how to abolish, dismantle, disassemble, and demolish oppression from our lives. As we have seen, depression is not oppression. Depression is physical and can be caused by disappointment, fatigue, our schedule, stress, or diet. Sometimes depression can be cured by medication, taking a day off, or changing your environment. Depression can become severe, and if not dealt with, oppression can enter into your life through that gate.

The word "oppression" originates from a Latin term which means *to press upon* or *to press against.* A person who is oppressed feels something pressing on him from the outside. Oppression does not come from the inside; it comes from the outside, and it is a spiritual force from the devil.

To oppress means *to overburden or weigh down.* When a person is oppressed, there is a feeling of being overwhelmed, overpowered, or weighed down. A person who is oppressed feels overpowered by his mind and emotions; the voice of the devil is overpowering him.

"Oppression" means *to burn with cruel, unjust or unreasonable restraint; to treat with severity.* A voice of oppression will restrain you and impose limitations on your life. Oppression also means *to oppress, afflict, crush, put down, smother, subdue or to torment.* Synonyms for the word oppression include, but are not limited to: *abuse, brutality, coercion, compulsion, conquering, and control.*

Oppression will control you. Through oppression, the devil tries to dictate what you are to feel and what you are to believe about your future and your identity. Oppression also carries the idea of *domination, force, harshness, harassment in the mind and emotions, hardness, injustice, ruling with an iron hand, maltreatment, overthrowing, repressing, suffering, severity, subjugation, torment, and tyranny.*

If you are a person who is oppressed, the devil is literally ruling over you like a tyrant. He has found a foothold into your mind, emotions, and imagination and has built a stronghold there. Like a wicked king or a wicked tyrant, from that stronghold, the devil is trying to dominate and control your life.

Weapons To Demolish Oppression

In Second Corinthians 10:4, Paul begins to explain how to demolish oppression.

> **For the weapons of our warfare are not carnal, but mighty through God to the pulling down of strong holds.**
> **— 2 Corinthians 10:4**

Paul begins this verse by discussing spiritual weapons. The Greek word for "weapons" in this verse is *hoopla*. It is from the word *hoplon* and describes the full weaponry that has been given to us by the Spirit of God. This weaponry is described explicitly in Ephesians chapter 6.

Ephesians 6:14 tells us God has given us the loin belt of truth and a breastplate of righteousness.

> **Stand therefore, having your loins girt about with truth, and having on the breastplate of righteousness....**

In verse 15, we find shoes of peace, which Rick calls "killer shoes."

> **And your feet shod with the preparation of the gospel of peace....**

In verse 16, we find the shield of faith.

> **Above all, taking the shield of faith, wherewith ye shall be able to quench all the fiery darts of the wicked.**

This means if your shield of faith is in place, the lies of the enemy will never penetrate your mind or your emotions.

In verse 17, we find the helmet of salvation and the sword of the Spirit.

> **And take the helmet of salvation, and the sword of the Spirit, which is the word of God....**

Finally, in verse 18, we find the lance of intercession.

> **Praying always with all prayer and supplication in the Spirit....**

In this passage, we find the full weaponry given to us by the Spirit of God. Those weapons are available to any believer to access and use against the oppression of the enemy.

A Well-Planned Strategy

Paul continues in Second Corinthians 10:4 and says, "For the weapons of our warfare...." The word "warfare" is the Greek word *strateia*, which describes *a well-planned strategic attack*. It is from the Greek word *streateuomai*, which depicts strategic warfare, including a line of attack, methods to be used in the attack, and the route chosen to carry out the debilitating assault.

If the enemy has tried to build a stronghold in your mind, you have access to spiritual weapons, and the Holy Spirit will give you a strategy — a well-planned route of attack for a debilitating assault — to pull down those strongholds.

The Bible also says that the weapons of our warfare are not *carnal*. The Greek word for "carnal" means *not fleshly* or *not from the material realm*. It literally means that these weapons are not natural; the use of these weapons cannot be taught by humans. They are of supernatural origin — divine spiritual weapons — and they are mighty.

The word "mighty" is the Greek word *dunatos*, which is from the word *dunamis*. It describes something explosive. It is superhuman power that comes with enormous energy and produces phenomenal, extraordinary, unparalleled results. It is the same Greek word that describes the full might of an advancing army, which means when these weapons are working, it is like an army's power has been released to drive back the darkness that has tried to attack your mind.

This passage continues by stating that those weapons are *mighty through God to the pulling down of strongholds.* Even the word "to" is important in Greek. It is the word *pros* and describes a face-to-face confrontation. This means when the weapons of God and the power of God are working in us, we no longer need to hide from the enemy; we can both confront the stronghold and pull it down. We are talking about demolishing oppression! "Pulling down" in Greek means *to take down; to disassemble, if needed, bit by bit.*

If you have a lie that has been working in your mind for a long time, you might need to untie it one little piece at a time, bit by bit. You have weapons and power to confront the lies, and you can begin to dismantle it; you can destroy it, throw it down, knock it down, break it up, pull it apart, and break it into pieces until nothing is left of the lie. The Greek word for "pulling down" is used to depict the pulling down of the walls of a well-defended fortress.

Stronghold Fortresses

The Greek word for "stronghold" is *ochuroma* and is very important. It describes a castle or a prison, a fortress. The Greek word pictures a stronghold with walls fortified to keep outsiders *out.* It also depicts a dreadful prison constructed deep inside a fortress that was intended to prevent a hostage or prisoner from escaping. It was a place of arrest, captivity, confinement, detention, imprisonment, or incarceration. It kept people *in.*

When the devil has built a stronghold in your mind or your emotions, it is like a castle. Who lives in castles? Kings. The devil, like a tyrant, moves into the lie that he has built, like a fortress, inside your head. It is a well-defended lie that you have heard for so long, you really believe it. Because you have believed the lie, it has empowered the lie to become a reality. When we embrace the lie the devil has been pounding into our thoughts, the devil moves in and, like a wicked king or tyrant, begins dominating our lives. Those negative thoughts become a well-defended lie. The lie becomes a fortress, a prison, and because the walls are so thick and you have been restrained by them for so long, when others try to help you, they cannot seem to penetrate the walls. You have been taken hostage and are imprisoned inside the walls of a well-defended lie in your head — a *stronghold.*

Casting Down Imaginations

Casting down imaginations, and every high thing that exalteth itself against the knowledge of God, and bringing into captivity every thought to the obedience of Christ.

— 2 Corinthians 10:5

This verse begins, "Casting down imaginations...." The phrase "casting down" is a translation of the same Greek word used for "pulling down" in verse 4. This means you can take it down and disassemble it if needed, bit by bit. The lie can be *demolished, destroyed, dismantled, thrown down, knocked down, broken up, broken apart, and pulled to pieces until nothing is left of it.* The Greek word describes pulling down the walls of a well-defended fortress. Paul makes it clear that he is referring to imaginations in this verse. In Greek, the word "imagination" is *logismos* and is where we get logical thinking. It denotes the thoughts and emotions operating in the mind. The mind is where strongholds take place. And the mind is where oppression occurs. The devil knows that the mind is the central control center of your life, and whoever controls your *mind* controls *you*. If the devil can control your mind, he can control what you think and what you believe. If he can control your mind, he can control your self-image. Your self-image will begin to affect the way you relate to others and how others perceive you.

Again, whoever has your mind has *you*. That is why *God* wants your mind! That's the reason we need to renew our mind with the Word of God (*see* Romans 12:2). God wants your mind because when God has your mind, He has *you*.

In the previous lesson, we discussed logical and illogical strongholds. But whether a stronghold is logical or illogical, it has the same effect. It is *a prison*. But the Bible says you can cast down that imagination — you can take it apart, dismantle it, and disassemble it, bit by bit, until nothing is left of it and you are finally free.

Not only can we *cast down imaginations*, Paul says we can cast down *every high thing that exalts itself against the knowledge of God*. The phrase "high thing" is from a Greek word describing any kind of barrier or any presumptuous thought. The Greek word for "exalts itself" describes *something haughty; something arrogant; something which, in pride, lifts itself up.*

An All-Out War Against the Knowledge of God

There is a Greek phrase for "against the knowledge of God" that is a combination of several different words. It depicts knowledge that defines its origin in God or a clear knowledge that comes from God. In Greek, when all of these words are put together for "against the knowledge of God," they depict an all-out war against the knowledge of God.

Let me give you an example: God says you are healed. This is the knowledge of God. Your flesh says you are not healed and you will never be healed. God also says you are perfect in Christ. Your flesh will say you are a failure and that you're never going to be anything in life. Your mind, your imagination that has been penetrated by the enemy, will exalt itself against whatever God says about you. God speaks the truth; oppression says the opposite. It is an all-out war against whatever God has declared about you!

What God has said about you is the truth. But if you are taken captive by oppression, by a stronghold or a vain imagination, your mind will wage war against the truth. If you want to be set free, you have to make a decision. Whatever oppression or stronghold or vain imagination is working in your head, you must decide to commit all-out war against that lie — that vain imagination.

Bring Every Thought Captive — *This Is War!*

Paul says you need to bring every thought captive to the obedience of Christ. The word "obedience" is the Greek word *hupakoe*. The word *hupo* carries the idea of being in a subservient position. The word *akoe* means *I hear*. When the two words are compounded, it depicts *one who is submitted; one who listens willingly or by force; one who obeys what he hears, either willingly or by compulsion, duress, or pressure.* To destroy strongholds, we must speak to our minds and emotions. In other words, *hupo*, you will submit yourself to the Word of God; *akoe*, you will decide to hear what God has to say and then obey that. You will believe and put into action what God says and not what you feel or the lie you have believed. You are going to *hupo* — submit your mind and your emotions — and *akoe*, you will listen and put into practice everything God says about you. In the process of making your mind and emotions submit to Christ and His

Word rather than to the life, you begin to disassemble those lies bit by bit and to demolish oppression in your life.

We must choose what voice we will listen to. We can either listen to the lie or listen to the truth. Whatever voice we listen to is the one we will believe, and the voice we believe is the one that will become our reality.

If you want to be free, you must listen to the freeing voice of God. If you want to be all that God says you are, you must listen to voice of God. That means you have to disassemble the other voice. You must bring every thought into captivity to the obedience of Christ and the knowledge of God — you must bring your mind captive to what *God* says about you. You must make the choice to hear the truth and believe it so that truth becomes your reality and obliterates the lie.

You can walk free of every oppressive thought if you are willing to listen to the Word of God and to cast down vain imaginations.

STUDY QUESTIONS

> **Study to shew thyself approved unto God, a workman that**
> **needeth not to be ashamed, rightly dividing the word of truth.**
> **— 2 Timothy 2:15**

1. Describe the weapons you have been given as found in Ephesians Chapter 6. Think about how you will use those weapons against future attacks.
2. In building your weapons arsenal, find one scripture in each area below:
   a. For healing.
   b. For peace.
   c. For provision.

PRACTICAL APPLICATION

> **But be ye doers of the word, and not hearers only,**
> **deceiving your own selves.**
> **— James 1:22**

1. Is there an area in your life where you are consciously or unconsciously fighting against the knowledge of God in your life? Really

think about it. Pray and ask the Lord to show you where you have been fighting against the knowledge of Him. Once He has revealed that area, make a determination to increase your knowledge of God's Word. Meditate on His Word; speak His Word over your life. It may take some time, but record a specific area where you have overcome because of this practice.

TOPIC

An Extreme Case of Oppression

SCRIPTURES

1. **Acts 10:38** — How God anointed Jesus of Nazareth with the Holy Ghost and with power: who went about doing good, and healing all that were oppressed of the devil; for God was with him.

2. **Mark 5:1-13** — And they came over unto the other side of the sea, into the country of the Gadarenes. And when he was come out of the ship, immediately there met him out of the tombs a man with an unclean spirit, who had his dwelling among the tombs; and no man could bind him, no, not with chains: Because that he had been often bound with fetters and chains, and the chains had been plucked asunder by him, and the fetters broken in pieces: neither could any man tame him. And always, night and day, he was in the mountains, and in the tombs, drying, and cutting himself with stones. But when he saw Jesus afar off, he ran and worshipped him, and cried with a loud voice, and said, What have I to do with thee, Jesus, thou Son of the most high God? I adjure thee by God, that thou torment me not. For he said unto him, Come out of the man, thou unclean spirit. And he asked him, What is thy name? And he answered, saying, my name is Legion: for we are many. And he besought him much that he would not send them away out of the country. And all the devils besought him saying, Send us into the swine, that we may enter into them. And forthwith Jesus gave them leave. And the unclean spirits went out, and entered into the swine: and the herd ran violently down a steep place into the sea, (they were about two thousand;) and were choked in the sea. And they that fed the swine fled, and told it in the city, and

in the country. And they went out to see what it was that was done. And they come to Jesus, and see him that was possessed with the devil, and had the legion, sitting, and clothed, and in his right mind: and they were afraid.

GREEK WORDS

1. "immediately" — εὐθὺς (*euthus*): without delay; immediately
2. "met" — ὑπαντάω (*hupantao*): to meet face to face; used militarily to denote a hostile meeting
3. "out" — ἐκ (*out*): out; where we get the word "exit"
4. "tombs" — μνῆμα (*mnema*): graves; tombs; tombstones
5. "with an unclean spirit" — ἐν πνεύματι ἀκαθάρτῳ (*en pneumati akatharto*): in the grip of an unclean spirit; in the control of an unclean spirit
6. "unclean" — ἀκάθαρτος (*akathartos*): unclean, impure, filthy, lewd, or foul
7. "dwelling" — κατοίκησις (*katoikesis*): to live among; to be housed among
8. "bind" — δέω (*deo*): to bind; tie up; restrict; imprison; put in chains
9. "chains" — ἅλυσις (*halusis*): chains or handcuffs for the hands or wrists
10. "fetters" — πέδη (*pede*): shackles on the feet; foot chains
11. "chains" — ἅλυσις (*halusis*): chains or handcuffs for the hands or wrists
12. "plucked asunder" — διασπάω (*diaspao*): to tear in half; to sever; to tear to pieces
13. "broken in pieces" — συντρίβω (*suntribo*): to crush, as in crushing bones or grapes; to smash
14. "tame" — δαμάζω (*damadzo*): a word that means to domesticate, to subdue, or to bring under control; used to describe animal trainers who were experts at capturing and domesticating the wildest and most ferocious beasts, such as lions, tigers, and bears; normally, these animals would maul or kill a person, but skilled trainers were able to take the wildest animals and domesticate them

15. "always, night and day" — διὰ παντὸς νυκτὸς καὶ ἡμέρας (*dia pantos nuktos kai hemeras*): constantly, throughout nighttime and daytime; perpetually, when it is dark and when it is light

16. "crying" — κράζω (*kradzo*): pictures an agonizing scream

17. "cutting" — κατακόπτω (*katakopto*): to cut downward; to gash downward; to mutilate

18. "ran" — τρέχω (*trecho*): to run swiftly; to run speedily, without distraction

19. "worshipped" — προσκυνέω (*proskuneo*): to fall forward to kiss; to fall upon on one's knees in adoration

20. "adjure" — ὁ ρκίζω (*horkidzo*): to solemnly plead; used in a religious sense to plead to God

21. "torment" — βασανίζω (*basanidzo*): torment or torture; however, the form used in this verse denotes incessant torment and torture

22. "said" — ἔλεγεν (*elegen*): the tense means, "He kept on, repeatedly saying..."

23. "out" — ἐκ (*ek*): out; where we get the word "exit"

24. "asked" — ἐπερωτάω (*eperotao*): to interrogate; tense depicts an ongoing interrogation

25. "legion" — λεγιὼν (*legion*): a military term; at least 6,000 Roman soldiers

26. "swine" — χοῖρος (*choiros*): the plural form for a pig or hog, which was considered to be the lowest, basest, and most unclean of animals

27. "went out" — ἐξέρχομαι (*exerchomai*): to come out; to make an exit

28. "entered" — εἰσέρχομαι (*eiserchoma*): to enter into; to travel into; to go into

29. "ran violently down" — ὁρμάω (*hormao*): to uncontrollably and wildly rush forward

30. "choked" — πνίγω (*pnigo*): to choke; to strangle; to wring the neck; to take one by the throat

31. "right mind" — σωφρονοῦντα (*sophronounta*): to be of sound mind; to be reasonable; to be balanced and levelheaded in the way one thinks; to think rationally; the tense means he was continuously in his right mind

SYNOPSIS

Moscow was already 300 years old when the Novospassky Monastery was constructed. It was a place where the religious worked and where people came to worship. Even in the Fourteenth century, it was a very historical place in Russia. Many notable people, including Romanovs, were buried behind these walls.

In 1917, the Bolshevik Revolution — also known as the Russian Revolution — occurred. The Bolsheviks did not believe in God. In fact, they were atheists and were "anti-religion" in their ideology. All places where religion was practiced were closed and religious workers were executed. When this particular monastery had been vacated and the religious workers had been executed, it became one of the first "shooting monasteries" in Moscow. In other words, it became a concentration camp. No one on the outside could see what was happening behind the walls of the monastery, but behind these walls people were tortured for their faith. If someone had a different political idea, they were incarcerated and brutalized. Eventually, it became a place of mass executions, horrible torture, and oppression.

In 1991, God moved in Russia and everything gloriously changed. God began to pour out His Spirit. From that time until now, Novospassky Monastery is once again a working monastery.

But what about oppressed people today? They may not be living behind the walls of a concentration camp, but they are bound by oppression nevertheless. They know something is wrong, but they may not realize that it is oppression. They don't know why they're oppressed or how to get free. In this lesson, we will examine how to heal people who are oppressed.

The emphasis of this lesson:

Regardless of the degree of oppression, freedom is available.

Seized With Oppression: An Extreme Case

In our study of *Healing the Mind and Emotions of the Oppressed*, we have examined oppression, its various levels, and how to demolish the strongholds of oppression. In this lesson, we are going to look at the example of a man who was severely oppressed. If it would have been impossible for someone not to ever be set free, it would have been this man. But this man actually wanted to be set free, and because he wanted to be set free, he *was* set free! *If you want to be free, you can be free too.*

Mark 5 records one of the most extreme cases of oppression found in the *New Testament.* Mark 5:1-3 says, "And they came over unto the other side of the sea, into the country of the Gadarenes. And when he [Jesus] was come out of the ship, immediately there met him out of the tombs a man with an unclean spirit, who had his dwelling among the tombs; and no man could bind him, no, not with chains...."

Verse 2 tells us a lot about this man. It says, "When he [Jesus] was come out of the ship, immediately there met him out of the tombs a man with an unclean spirit." When the Bible uses the word "immediately," it is a Greek word meaning *without delay.*

Immediately after Jesus got out of the boat, this man charged out of the tombs. In fact, the Bible says, "...There met him...." The Greek word for "met" usually denotes a hostile meeting. It says, "...There met him *out of the tombs....*" The word "out" is the Greek word *ek,* which means he made an exit directly out of the tombs. This man was living among the tombs. The Bible says he had an unclean spirit. The Greek literally says *he was in the grip or control of an unclean spirit.* The man didn't have a spirit — that *spirit* had *him.* This was a man that was *seized* with oppression. What began as a stronghold became *possession.*

Even the word "unclean" is important because it describes something *unclean, impure, lewd, filthy, and foul.* This word describes the nature of evil spirits. They are lewd, vile, filthy, and foul — and this man was in the grip of that spirit. Some believe this may insinuate the man had played with wrong thoughts — unclean thoughts — for so long that it opened the door for this satanic affliction to come into his life.

Dwelling Among the Tombs

Verse 3 says this "seized" man had his dwelling among the tombs. The word "dwelling" literally means *to be housed among.* This man was closer to death than he was to life. Thoughts of death were on his mind. Those thoughts of death began to seize him; they began to fill his mind until he was no longer living in his house, and he did have a house. This chapter tells us that when he was set free, he was sent home to his friends (v. 19). But under this demonic oppression, he had left his house and was living in the vicinity of death. Death was on his mind, and he was literally housed among the tombs.

Verse 3 continues, "…No man could bind him, no not with chains." The word "bind" is the Greek word *deo*, which means *to bind or to incarcerate*. The word "chains" is the Greek word describing *chains or handcuffs for the hands or the wrists*.

Verse 4 continues, "Because that he had been often bound with fetters and chains.…" The phrase "often bound" means people had already attempted to bind him on multiple occasions, but they could not keep this man bound. The word "fetters" is a Greek word describing chains or cuffs that are wrapped around the feet. This man was literally bound hand and foot.

He Could Not Be Tamed

Again, verse 4 says, "…And the chains had been plucked asunder by him and the fetters broken in pieces." The phrase "plucked asunder" means *to tear in half; to sever into two pieces*. The particular chain mentioned in this verse was a solid band of metal that went around both of his hands. This man was so demonically energized, he had the strength to *pluck it asunder* or *to rip it in half, severing it into two pieces*.

The fetters on his feet he had broken into pieces. The Greek word for "broken in pieces" is *suntribo*, which means *to crush or grind to dust*. It is the same word used to describe the smashing of grapes into wine or the grinding of bones into dust. This man could rub his feet together so demonically, so powerfully, that he could reduce the metal to dust. This man severed the metal on his hands, reduced the metal on his ankles to dust, and the Bible says, "…Neither could any man tame him…." The word "tame" is the Greek word *damadzo*, and it means *to domesticate, to subdue, or to bring under control*. This very word for "tame" is also used to describe animal trainers who are experts at capturing and domesticating the wildest and most ferocious beasts, including lions, tigers, and bears. It was not uncommon for these animals to maul or kill humans. Skilled trainers were able to take the wildest animals and domesticate them, but not this man; he could not be subdued or controlled. He could not be domesticated or "tamed."

Death-Filled Thoughts

A study of this text is quite amazing. This was a man who was in the grip of an unclean spirit. His mind was so filled with oppression and consumed with thoughts of death, he had left his home. Those thoughts had driven him into the graveyard where he was housed among the tombs. This man was in the grip of a foul, unclean, filthy spirit, which may have entered through the avenue of unclean thinking. This is what the Greek implies. Men had to bind him with handcuffs and had tried to bind his feet, yet he had ripped the handcuffs into pieces and ground the fetters on his feet into pieces. Then they brought wild-animal tamers in to try to domesticate him, and those who could tame the wildest and most ferocious beasts had no success. That is how wild and oppressed this man was.

Verse 5 says, "And always, night and day, he was in the mountains, and in the tombs, crying, and cutting himself with stones."

When the Bible says "always night and day," the Greek literally means *always; constantly; throughout the nighttime and throughout the daytime* or *perpetually, when it was dark and when it was light.* It didn't matter what time of the day it was, this man was in the tombs nestled in the vicinity of death.

Verse 5 reveals the man was crying. The Greek word for crying is *kradzo*, which depicts *an agonizing scream.* This man was really tortured; he was under the power of oppression. The devil was controlling him, and the man was so miserable, he was crying out with an agonizing scream.

The Bible also says he was cutting himself with stones. The Greek word for "cutting" is *katakopto*, meaning *a downward gash.* There are two possibilities of meaning here: 1) He may have been trying to commit suicide or, 2) he may have been trying to liberate himself of these demon spirits. This man was truly tormented.

Running Toward Freedom

Notice what verse 6 says, "But when he saw Jesus afar off, he ran and worshipped him...." The word "ran" is a Greek word *trecho*, which means *to run swiftly, to run speedily without distraction.* The man raced toward Jesus when he saw Him. He dashed out of the tombs as fast as he could. The word *trecho* means *to move your feet so quickly they are barely hitting the ground.* This man was moving as fast as he could to get to Jesus. In fact, the verse says he *worshiped* Him. The Greek word for "worshiped" is *proskuneo*. It is a combination of *pros*, which means *forward*, and *kuneo*, which means *to kiss*. This man made a dive toward Jesus. If he was really that oppressed — if he was so possessed and full of the devil — why wouldn't he run *away* from Jesus rather than *toward* Him? The explanation for this is recorded in Luke 8:29.

> **For he [Jesus] had commanded the unclean spirit to come out of the man. For oftentimes it had caught him: and he was kept bound with chains and fetters; and he brake the bands, and it was driven of the devil into the wilderness.**

Luke, the physician, tells us that from time to time the spirit would *catch* this man, or according to the Greek, *seize him by force*. It is the same identical Greek word used to describe epilepsy. This does not mean the man had epilepsy, but this demonic manifestation behaved like epilepsy.

Think about epilepsy for a moment. If a person has been diagnosed with epilepsy, he doesn't live in a continual state of seizures. In fact, sometimes you don't even know the person has dealt with epilepsy because he moves so normally. But then, suddenly, he has an epileptic seizure.

This passage indicates that there were times when this man was in his right mind and then, suddenly, the demon would seize him and throw him into a fit. When Jesus had come to the other side of the lake, as recorded in Mark 5:1 and 2, and encountered this man with an unclean spirit, at that particular moment, the man was in control of himself. He was still living among the tombs and was in very bad shape, but the demonic powers had subsided. When the man saw Jesus, he recognized Him and ran toward Him. This was a man who truly wanted to be set free.

Again, Mark 5:6 says, "But when he saw Jesus afar off, he ran and worshipped Him." Again, the Greek word for "worshiped" is *proskuneo*, meaning *to kiss, like a dog licking his master's hand*. This man took a dive toward Jesus and was expressing himself the best that he was able. He made a dash for Jesus, worshiping Him, and as he lifted his voice to speak, the demon spirits caught him. Rather than expressing himself, the demons began to speak through him.

The Devil Prayed!

Mark 7 continues describing what happened. "And [the demons] cried with a loud voice, and said, What have I do to with thee, Jesus, thou Son of the most high? I adjure thee by God, that thou torment me not." The word "adjure" is a religious term, which means *to pray*. I refer to this incident as the day the devil prayed!

The devil is now praying! The word "torment" is the Greek word *basanidzo*, meaning *to torture* or *to torment*. But the form used in this passage describes *incessant torment; incessant torture*. Jesus was doing something that caused this demon to cry out, *Stop tormenting me!* What was Jesus doing? Mark 5:8 tells us. "For he [Jesus] said unto him, Come out of the man, thou unclean spirit."

The Greek word for "said" indicates that Jesus kept *repeatedly* saying. This means the first time Jesus spoke to these demons, they didn't come out. But Jesus didn't walk away in defeat. He just kept persistently commanding, "Come out! Come out! Come out!" When He said, "Come out," the Greek word for "out" is the word *ek*. It means *to make an exit*. Jesus was saying, "I'm not leaving until you exit this man, you unclean spirit!"

Again, the Greek meaning indicates Jesus was saying, "You foul, stinking, filthy, vile thing, I am commanding you to make an exit!" Jesus kept saying and kept saying and kept saying.

Religious leaders had given up and walked away.

Those who bound prisoners gave up and walked away.

Those who tamed wild animals gave up and walked away.

But not Jesus.

Jesus said, "I am not leaving until this man's desire has been met." When he ran toward Jesus, the man expressed his desire. He was doing the best he could do to say by his actions, "I want to be free!"

Finally, in verse 9, Jesus asked the demon its name. The Greek actually says that Jesus *interrogated* him.

> **And he asked him, What is thy name? And he [the demon] answered, saying, My name is Legion: for we are many.**

The word "Legion" is a military term, which denotes *at least 6,000 in number.* That's 6,000 demons or evil spirits! Now notice their response to Jesus in verses 10 through 12: "And he [that is the demon who was speaking] besought him much that he would not send them away out of the country. Now there was there nigh unto the mountains a great herd of swine feeding. And *all the devils* besought him, saying, Send us into the swine, that we may enter into them."

The word "swine" is the plural version for *a pig* or *a hog*, which were considered to be the lowest, basest, and most unclean of animals. Verse 12 reveals that suddenly "all the devils" began speaking. Six thousand evil spirits were now simultaneously speaking through the man's mouth. Imagine what that would have sounded like! "And all the devils besought Him saying send us into the pigs, into the hogs, that we may enter into them." These demons were so foul, they were even willing to live in a hog, the most base and unclean of animals!

> **And forthwith Jesus gave them leave. And the unclean spirits went out, and entered into the swine: and the herd ran violently down a steep place into the sea, (they were about two thousand;) and were choked in the sea.**
>
> **— Mark 5:13**

The Will To Be Free

When the Bible says this herd of swine "ran violently" down the mountain, it means *they ran uncontrollably and wildly rushed forward.* The phrase "choked in the sea" means they were choking before they even got into the sea. The word *choked* means *to strangle or to take somebody by the neck.* This man was not killed by the demons. He was living in the vicinity of death, he was housed among the tombs, he was crying in agony, he was cutting himself with stones, and he was living a miserable existence. Yet the demons were not able to destroy him. Why? Because he had a mind and he had a will. This man did not want to be destroyed. As long as you have a will to be set free, you can resist anything that is working in your mind and in your emotions.

This man with the unclean spirit was demonstrating his will when he ran toward Jesus, even though he was confused, and even though the demons spoke through him. Jesus recognized that this man was demonstrating a fierce desire to be set free. Jesus responded by saying, "I am not leaving this man until he is liberated." That is the reason Jesus kept saying and saying and saying, "Come out!"

In other words, "Make an exit! I am not leaving until you come out of this man!" And Jesus cast the demons out of the man. The demons entered the herd of swine, which immediately ran into the sea. Verses 14 and 15 read: "And they that fed the swine fled, and told it in the city, and in the country. And they went out to see what it was that was done. And they come to Jesus, and see him that was possessed with the devil, and had the legion, sitting, and clothed, and in his right mind: and they were afraid."

This man who had been so bound was now sitting, clothed, and completely normal and in his right mind. The phrase "right mind" means *to be of sound mind; to be reasonable; to be balanced and levelheaded in the way one thinks; to think rationally.* In Greek, the tense means *he was continuously in his right mind from that moment forward.*

If you are one of those who say, "I just can't control my mind, and I just can't control my emotions," you need to quit lying to yourself. You have the ability to resist wrong thoughts and emotions. You can get to Jesus and you can apply the Word of God. If this man, who had a legion of demons, could make a dash toward Jesus and be set free, anybody can be set free! There is hope for anyone — for you, for your child, for your grandchild, for your friends and loved ones. Jesus will stay with *anyone* who will make a dash toward Him until their mind and their emotions are liberated — until they are set free and healed!

STUDY QUESTIONS

Study to shew thyself approved unto God, a workman that needeth not to be ashamed, rightly dividing the word of truth.
— 2 Timothy 2:15

1. After studying this story about the man from the Gadarenes in Mark 5:1-13, what have you learned about God's ability to look beyond the outward condition to the heart of an individual and about God's great love for people, even the most hopeless and bound? What have you learned about yourself from examining this story?

PRACTICAL APPLICATION

**But be ye doers of the word, and not hearers only,
deceiving your own selves.
—James 1:22**

1. Think about a time you may have judged someone based on his outward appearance and behavior. Be honest. Were you tempted to think, *I'm not sure if there is hope for that guy!* Ask God to help you see individuals through His eyes, with His heart, and according to His Word. Read First Corinthians 13 out loud.

LESSON 5

TOPIC

Ministering to the Oppressed

SCRIPTURES

1. **Luke 10:17-19** — And the seventy returned again with joy, saying, Lord, even the devils are subject unto us through thy name. And he said unto them, I beheld Satan as lightening fall from heaven. Behold, I give unto you power to tread on serpents and scorpions, and over all the power of the enemy...

2. **Isaiah 14:12** — How art thou fallen from heaven, O Lucifer, con of the morning! How art though cut down to the ground, which didst weaken the nations!

3. **Ezekiel 28:16** — By the multitude of thy merchandise they have filled the midst of thee with violence, and thou hast sinned: therefore I will cast thee as profane out of the mountain of God: and I will destroy thee, O covering cherub, from the midst of the stones of fire.

4. **Acts 10:38** — How God anointed Jesus of Nazareth with the Holy Ghost and with power: who went about doing good, and healing all that were oppressed of the devil; for God was with him.

5. **1 John 2:20** — But ye have an unction from the Holy One...

GREEK WORDS

1. "devils" — δαιμόνια (*daimonia*): evil spirits; demons; devils; the ancient world believed demons populated the lower regions of the air and that they were the primary cause of disasters and suffering; depicts a person deemed mentally sick or insane; in the New Testament, δαιμόνια (*daimonia*) depicts those having mental sicknesses or physical infirmities that are spirit-inflicted

2. "subject" — ὑποτάσσω (*hupotasso*): used militarily to depict a soldier who falls in line when a commander gives an order; pictures one submitted to authority

3. "beheld" — θεωρέω (*theoreo*): to gaze at; to look upon; it's the root word for "theater"

4. "behold" — ἰδού (*idou*): bewilderment, shock, amazement, and wonder

5. "power" — ἐξουσία (*exousia*): authority; denotes one who has received delegated power

6. "tread" — πατέω (*pateo*): to walk on; to trample, to crush; to advance by setting the foot upon

7. "serpents" — ὄφις (*ophis*): a serpent; snake; used of the devil or Satan

8. "scorpions" — σκορπίος (*skorpios*): a scorpion; a creature with a poisonous sting

9. "over" — ἐπὶ (*epi*): over; denotes a position of advantage and superiority

10. "power" — δύναμις (*dunamis*): power; dynamic power; superhuman power; depicts the full force of an advancing army

11. "enemy" — ἐχθρός (*echthros*): enemy; someone who is openly hostile; one with a deep-seated hatred; an irreconcilable hostility; one who is bent on inflicting harm

12. "power" — δύναμις (*dunamis*): power; pictures explosive, superhuman power that comes with enormous energy and produces phenomenal, extraordinary, and unparalleled results; used to depict the full might and power of an advancing army

13. "healing" — ἰάομαι (*iaomai*):to cure; to be doctored; pictures healing power that progressively reverses a condition; denotes healing that comes to pass over a period of time; for this reason, this word is often translated as a treatment, cure, or remedy; depicts a sickness that has been progressively healed rather than instantaneously healed

14. "oppressed" — **καταδυναστεύω** (*katadunasteuo*): a compound of **κατα** (kata) and **δυνάστης** (*dunastes*); the word **κατα** (kata) carries the idea of domination; the word **δυνάστης** (*dunastes*) depicts a dominating tyrant; when compounded, it pictures the oppressive power of a wicked tyrant; one who rules over and cruelly tyrannizes his subjects; bullying; cruelty; despotism; dictatorship; oppressiveness; tyranny

15. "devil" — **διάβολος** (*diabolos*): one who repetitiously strikes until successfully penetrating an object to ruin it, affect it, or take it captive; to slander, accuse, or defame; to penetrate by continuous assault; to ensnare with a net

16. "unction" — **χρίσμα** (*chrisma*): the anointing; to be smeared and covered with the anointing

SYNOPSIS

As mentioned previously, the Novospassky Monastery in Moscow is a historical location in the city, first constructed in the Fourteenth Century as a working monastery, but closed in 1917 because of the Bolshevik Revolution. The Bolsheviks and early communists were atheistic. They were against all forms of religion, and the monastery closed because religion became illegal. Prisoners were incarcerated there, and this site eventually became a concentration camp where there were mass executions for people of faith and people with differing political views.

Behind the walls of this monastery horrible things happened; it became a place of torture and oppression. Thankfully, today it is once again a functioning monastery, a cathedral where people come to worship in the new Russia. It is so wonderful what God has done in Russia. However, during the early years of the Soviet regime, this was a place of horrific oppression.

If you have ever dealt personally with oppression or know someone struggling with it, you understand how horrible it is. Maybe you haven't known how to help someone struggling with oppression, but there is a way to minister to those who are oppressed to help bring freedom.

The emphasis of this lesson:

In our final lesson, we will learn about the authority we have been given to overcome the devil and set others free who have been bound by oppression.

Review: Depression Is Not Oppression

In review, there is a difference between depression and oppression. Depression can be both physical and emotional. It can be caused by a disappointment, fatigue, stress, diet, or chemical imbalance. Depression can be remedied by making adjustments in our lives or by medication.

Rick related in this program that he suffered a bout of depression as a result of a wrong, grueling schedule. When he fixed his schedule, the depression disappeared. Another time earlier in his life, he dealt with depression and discovered it was triggered by sugar. When he eliminated sugar from his diet, the depression went away.

Depression is physically curable. Oppression is different from depression; it is not physical, but spiritual. Oppression originates from an outside spiritual source.

The word "oppression" indicates the exercise of authority or power in a burdensome or cruel or unjust way. It means *to press upon*; *to press against*; *to overburden*; *to weigh down*; *to overwhelm*; and *to overpower*. It also means to burden, to be unjust, to be cruel, to exercise uncontrollable restraints, to treat with severity, to oppress, to afflict, to crush, to put down, to smother, to subdue, or to torment.

Oppression is an exterior spiritual force that tries to control you. Oppression tries to quell, smother, and control you. The devil tries to suppress our lives so we will not become what God desires us to be. Other synonyms for oppression include: abuse, brutality, coercion, compulsion, conquering, control, cruelty, despotism, dictatorship, domination, force, harshness, harassment, hardness, injustice, ruling with an iron hand, maltreatment, overthrowing, repression, suffering, severity, subjugation, torment, and tyranny.

These words vividly describe what oppression does in a person's life.

We have come to our final lesson in the series *Healing the Mind and Emotions of the Oppressed.* In the first lesson, we identified oppression. In the second lesson, we examined the seven levels of oppression. In lesson three, we learned how to demolish oppression; how to dismantle it if need be, piece by piece, to walk free of it. In lesson four, we studied a severe case of oppression described in Mark, Chapter 5, the demoniac of Gadara. That man was so oppressed, he was in the *grip* of an unclean spirit. He actually had 6,000 demons, but when he saw Jesus, he made a dash for Him to get help. This story reveals that it doesn't matter how bad your situation is, you have the ability to express your desire to be set free.

In our final lesson, we will discover how to minister to others who are oppressed.

Authority in His Name

Luke 10:17 records the account of Jesus sending the 70 disciples out to minister.

And the seventy returned again with joy, saying, Lord, even the devils [spirits] are subject unto us through thy name.

Jesus had sent the 70 out with authority to heal and to cast out demons. They were so excited, when they returned, they said, "…Lord, even the spirits, the devils are subject unto us through thy name." The word "devils" is the Greek word *daimonia*. This word describes *evil spirits, demons, or devils*. The ancient world believed demons populated the lower regions of the air and were the primary cause of disasters and suffering. They were correct. In the New Testament, this word *daimonia*, or devils, depicts those having mental illnesses, oppression or physical infirmities that are inflicted by evil spirits.

The word *daimonia* describes people who are oppressed, having spirit-inflicted issues in their mind or body. The Bible says when the 70 returned, they said, "Lord, the demons, these evil spirits, the source of all disaster and mental illness and struggling, are subject unto us through Your name."

The word "subject" is the Greek word *hupotasso*, which is a military term. It portrays *a soldier who falls in line when a commander gives an order; one who is submitted to authority*. These disciples said, "Lord, when we speak, they recognize our voices as the voices of commanders, and they fall in line when we use Your name!" In the same way, *you* have the name of Jesus and the authority designated to you by Jesus. When you speak, demon spirits — every foul, evil force — will hear the voice of a commander and fall in line when you use Jesus' name.

'I Saw Satan Fall Like Lightning'

In Luke 10:18 Jesus said, "I beheld Satan as lightning fall from heaven." The word "beheld" is the Greek word *theoreo*, which means *to gaze at* or *to look upon*. It is the root word from which we get the word *theater*. Jesus was literally saying, "Guys, I know you're impressed by what you've just experienced because demons respond to you when you speak, but let me tell you about My experience. I remember when Satan fell from Heaven like lightning." Jesus used the word "beheld," which means Jesus said, in effect, "I watched it like I was in a theater. I watched the first act, the second act, and the third act. I saw the entire show; I watched the whole event."

Portions of that event are recorded in Isaiah 14:12 and Ezekiel 28:16.

Isaiah 14:12

How art thou fallen from heaven, O Lucifer, son of the morning! How art thou cut down to the ground, which dost weaken the nations!

Lucifer fell from Heaven and was cut to the ground.

Ezekiel 28:16

…Therefore I will cast thee as profane out of the mountain of God.

Lucifer was cut to the ground; he fell from the heavens, cast out as profane. He fell so rapidly that Jesus said he fell *like lightning*. He was gone in a flash. Immediately after describing Lucifer's fall, Jesus says in Luke 10:19, "Behold…."

Authority To Trample Serpents and Scorpions

In Greek, the word "behold" is *idou*, which contains the idea of bewilderment, shock, amazement, and wonder. Jesus was so excited about what He was about to say that He began with the Greek word *idou*, which means *behold*. In essence, Jesus was saying, "Hey guys, this is amazing! What I'm about to tell you is phenomenal! *"Behold*, I give you power [authority] to trample on serpents and scorpions, and over all the power of the enemy.…"

The word for "power" is the Greek word *exousia* and it describes *one who has received delegated authority and power*. Jesus said, "I'm giving you authority; I'm delegating this authority to you to *tread*.…" The word "tread" is the Greek word *pateo* meaning *to walk on, to trample, to crush, to advance by setting the foot upon*. Jesus said, "I'm giving you power to advance, and along the way, if necessary, you can trample serpents and scorpions." The word "serpents" is the Greek word *ophis*, meaning *snake*. This word is used in the Scripture to describe Satan when he strikes to kill.

Jesus said, "You have no need to be afraid of the devil or any attack he may wage against you because I have given you authority to move your feet. Just start walking forward. If the devil gets in your way, trample him with no fear of an attack or of him striking you." The word "scorpion" is from the Greek word *skorpios*, which describes *a scorpion or a creature with a poisonous sting*. Jesus said, "You don't need to worry about being hurt or being stung because I've given you authority to make an advancement. Move your feet and just start marching forward, and if the devil or any stinging situation gets in your way, if anything comes to strike you or sting you, don't worry. Just move your feet, because I have given you authority to advance and to trample those serpents and scorpions along the way."

Jesus went on to say, "I've given you authority...over all the power of the enemy." The word "over" is the Greek word *epi*, which denotes *a position of advantage and superiority*. Because Jesus has given us authority, we have a position of advantage. We have a position of superiority over all the power of the enemy! *Wow!*

The Force of an Advancing Army

In this instance, the word "power" depicts *an advancing army*. The enemy tries to advance on us. It may appear as though Satan's troops are coming against us, but don't allow yourself to worry because you have authority over and have a position of advantage or superiority over the advancing power of the enemy. The word "enemy" that is used here is the Greek word *echthros*, which describes *someone who is openly hostile, one with deep-seated animosity and hatred, an irreconcilable hostility, or one who is bent on inflicting harm*. Jesus said, "Don't worry about him. I've given you authority over anything he can ever wage against you." That is why Jesus began by saying "Behold…" in Luke 10:19. Jesus said, "Wow! Isn't the authority I've given you amazing?"

Friend, *you* have been given authority over ALL the works of the enemy!

Returning to Acts 10:38, we read, "How God anointed Jesus of Nazareth with the Holy Spirit and with power…." The word "power" is the Greek word *dunamis*. It describes *explosive, superhuman power that comes with extraordinary, unparalleled results*. It's the same Greek word that describes the full might of an advancing army.

When Jesus was anointed, He had amazing, supernatural power with unparalleled results. When that power worked in Jesus, it was like the heavenly armies were unleashed. The power of God was moving forward to drive back the forces of evil, and that is why He went about doing good and healing all who were oppressed by the devil.

In this verse, the word "oppressed" is a compound of two Greek words, *kata* and *dunamis*. In this particular case, the word *kata* caries the idea of *domination*. The word *dunamis* depicts *a domineering tyrant*. It is a picture of the oppressive power of a wicked tyrant, one who rules cruelly and tyrannizes his subjects — one who is a cruel bully, dictator, or oppressive tyrant.

The word "devil," as mentioned previously, is the Greek word *diabolos*, describing *one who repetitiously strikes until successfully penetrating an object to ruin it, affect it, or take it captive*. It also means *to slander, accuse, defame, penetrate by continuous assault, or ensnare with a net*.

The devil wants to dominate your life; he wants to control your mind and emotions. He begins repeatedly striking the mind and the emotions until he finally moves in like a wicked tyrant and begins to tyrannize and rule over you like a wicked king.

But Jesus came with an anointing and with power to set at liberty all who are being tyrannized by the devil. If you know others who are subject to the cruel, oppressive treatment of the devil in their mind and emotions, pray for them, lay hands on them, and release the power of God because according to Luke 10, He gave us power over *all* the works of the enemy. You have a position of advantage and superiority, and if you will use your voice of authority and release the power of God through your hands, God will use you to bring freedom to those who are bound and to those who are oppressed of the devil.

You Have an Anointing

According to Acts 10:38, Jesus was anointed. The hand of God was upon Him. When the hand of God came upon Him, the power of God began to work in Him, which was able to set people free. But speaking of believers, First John 2:20 says, "But ye have an unction [anointing)] from the Holy One...." That word "unction" is the Greek word *chrisma*, and it means *anointing*. Specifically, it means that if you are in Christ, the anointing belongs to you; both legally and potentially, it is yours to experience. You are covered from head to toe with the same anointing that was upon Jesus. This means you have the same dynamic power, and just as Jesus "set at liberty them that were bruised" and delivered those who were oppressed by the devil, *you* can be used by God to speak a word of deliverance to people who are bound.

God wants to use you to help dismantle those strongholds and vain imaginations in their minds. God has given you a voice and hands to release power just like Jesus was anointed. First John 2:20 says you have received an *unction*, or *charisma*. You are anointed from top to bottom, from head to toe, with the same anointing that will bring freedom to anyone who is oppressed of the devil.

If you are oppressed, you can be set free. If you know someone who is subject to the tyrannizing voice of the enemy, it is time for them to be set free. Jesus may want to use you to minister liberty to them, and you can do it because you have an unction from the Holy One. The same anointing that was on Jesus is on you! *You can do it!*

STUDY QUESTIONS

Study to shew thyself approved unto God, a workman that needeth not to be ashamed, rightly dividing the word of truth.
— 2 Timothy 2:15

1. After Jesus described the fall of Satan in Luke 10:19, why was it significant that he said, "Behold..."? Explain.
2. In Luke 10:19, the word "power" is used twice. Define each instance of the word "power" in this verse.
    a. I give unto you *power* to tread....
    b. over all the *power* of the enemy....

PRACTICAL APPLICATION

But be ye doers of the word, and not hearers only, deceiving your own selves.
—James 1:22

1. First John 2:20 says that you have an *unction*. That means, you are *smeared and covered with the anointing from head to toe*. Think about how you are walking in that anointing to set at liberty those who are bound. How can you increase your effectiveness to free the captives in your world?

Notes

Notes

Notes

_____

_____

_____

_____

_____

_____

_____

_____

_____

_____

_____

_____

_____

_____

_____

_____

_____

_____

_____

_____

_____

_____

_____

_____

_____

_____

www.ingramcontent.com/pod-product-compliance
Lightning Source LLC
Chambersburg PA
CBHW051047030426
42339CB00006B/235